Healthy Instant Pot Meal Plan

Best Instant Pot 365 Days Meal Plan with Amazing Dishes, the Simple Way to Healthier Eating!

Adrian Marvin

Table of Contents

broadly considered a truthful and accurate account of facts and as such, any inattention, use, or misuse of the information in question by the reader will render any resulting actions solely under their purview. There are no scenarios in which the publisher or the original author of this work can be in any fashion deemed liable for any hardship or damages that may befall them after undertaking information described herein. Additionally, the information in the following pages is intended only for informational purposes and should thus be thought of as universal. As befitting its nature, it is presented without assurance regarding its prolonged validity or interim quality. Trademarks that are mentioned are done without written consent and can in no way be considered an endorsement from the trademark holder.

Introduction

Instant pot is a pressure cooker, also stir-fry, stew, and cook rice, cook vegetables and chicken. It's an all-in-one device, so you can season chicken and cook it in the same pan, for example. In most cases, instant pot meals can be served in less than an hour.

Cooking less time is due to the pressure cooking function that captures the steam generated by the liquid cooking environment (including liquids released from meat and vegetables), boosts the pressure and pushes the steam back.

But don't confuse with traditional pressure cookers. The instant pot, unlike the pressure cooker used by grandparents, eliminates the risk of safety with a lid that locks and remains locked until pressure is released.

Even when cooking time is over in the instant pot, you need to take an additional step-to release the pressure.

There are two ways to relieve pressure. Due to the natural pressure release, the lid valve remains in the sealing position and the pressure will naturally dissipate over time. This process takes 20 minutes to over an hour, depending on what is cooked. Low fluidity foods (such as chicken wings) take less time than high fluidity foods such as soups and marinades.

Another option is manual pressure release (also called quick release). Now you need to carefully move the valve to the ventilation position and see that the steam rises slowly and the pressure is released. This Directions is much faster, but foods with high liquid content, such as soups, take about 15 minutes to manually relieve pressure.

Which option should I use? Take into account that even if natural pressure is released, the instant pot is still under pressure. This means that the food will continue to cook while the instant pot is in sealed mode. Manual pressure relief is useful when the dishes are well cooked and need to be stopped as soon as possible.

If the goal is to prepare meals quickly, set the cooking time for dishes that are being cooked in an instant pop and release the pressure manually after the time has passed.

Instant pots (called "Instapot" by many) are one of our favorite cookware because they can handle such a wide range of foods almost easily. Instant pots range from those that work on the basics of pressure cooking to those that can be sterilized using Suicide video or some models can be controlled via Wi-Fi.

In addition, if you want to expand the range of kitchenware, the Instant Pot brand has released an air fryer that can be used to make rotisserie chicken and homemade beef jerky. There is also an independent accumulator device that can be used in instant pots to make fish, steaks and more.

The current icon instant pot works like a pressure cooker and uses heat and steam to quickly cook food. Everything from perfect carnitas to boiled eggs was cooked, but not all ingredients and DIRECTIONS work. Here are few foods that should not be cooked in classic instant pots.

Instant pots are not pressure fryer and are not designed to handle the high temperatures required to heat cooking oils like crispy fried chicken. Of course, the instant pot is great for dishes like Carnitas, but after removing the meat from the instant pot, to get the final crispness in the meat, transfer it to a frying pan for a few minutes or to an oven top and hot Crispy in the oven.

As with slow cookers, dairy products such as cheese, milk, and sour cream will pack into instant pots using pressure cooking settings or slow cooking settings. Do not add these ingredients after the dish are cooked or create a recipe in Instapot.

There are two exceptions. One is when making yogurt. This is merely possible if you are using an instant pot recipe. The other is only when making cheesecake and following an instant pot recipe.

Although you can technically cook pasta in an instant pot, gummy may appear and cooking may be uneven. To be honest, unless you have a choice, cooking pasta in a stove pot is just as fast and easy and consistently gives you better cooked pasta.

Instead of baking the cake in an instant pot, steam it. The cake is moist-it works for things like bread pudding-but there is no good skin on the cake or on the crunchy edge everyone fights with a baked brownie. However, let's say your desire is to build a close-up or a simple dessert with your family; you can get a damp sponge in about 30 minutes, except during the DIRECTIONS time.

Canning, a technique for cooking and sealing food in a jar, is often done in a pressure cooker. Therefore, it is recommended to create a batch of jam, pickles or jelly in Instapot. Please do not.

With an instant pot, you can't monitor the temperature of what you can, like a normal pressure cooker. In canning, it is important to cook and seal the dishes correctly. Incorrect cooking and sealing can lead to the growth of bacteria that can cause food poisoning.

If you want to avoid canning in an instant pot, some newer models, such as Duo Plus, have a sterilization setting that can clean kitchen items such as baby bottles, bottles and cookware.

Instant Pot Pressure Cooker Safety Tips

Instant Pot is a very safe pressure cooker consisting of various safety mechanisms. do not worry. It will not explode immediately. Most accidents are caused by user errors and can be easily avoided. To further minimize the possibility of an accident, we have compiled a list of safety tips.

1 Don't leave it alone

It is not recommended to leave home while cooking an instant pot. If you have to leave it alone, make sure it is under pressure and no steam is coming out.

2 Do not use KFC in instant pot

Do not fry in an instant pot or other pressure cooker.

KFC uses a commercial pressure fryer specially made to fry chicken (the latest one that operates at 5 PSI). Instant pots (10.5-11.6 PSI) are specially made to make our lives easier.

3 water intake!

Instant pots require a minimum of 1 1/2 cup liquid (Instant Pot Official Number) 1 cup liquid to reach and maintain pressure.

The liquid can be a combination of gravy, vinegar, water, chicken etc.

4 half full or half empty

The max line printed on the inner pot of the instant pot is not for pressure cooking.

For pressure cooking: up to 2/3 full

Food for pressure cooking that expands during cooking (grains, beans, dried vegetables, etc.): up to 1/2

5 Not a facial steamer

Deep cleaning is not performed even if the pressure cooker steam is used once.

When opening, always tilt the lid away from you. Wear waterproof and heat-resistant silicone gloves especially when performing quick release.

6 never use power

 In situations of zero, you should try to force open the lid of the instant pot pressure cooker, unless you want to prevent a light saber from hitting your face.

7 Wash Up & Checkout

If you want to be secured, wash the lid after each use and clean the anti-block shield and inner pot. Make sure that the gasket (silicon seal ring) is in good shape and that there is no food residue in the anti-block shield before use.

Usually silicone seal rings should be replaced every 18-24 months. It is always advisable to keep extra things.

Do not purchase a sealing ring from a third party because it is an integral part of the safety features of the instant ring.

Using sealing rings that have not been tested with instant pot products can create serious safety concerns."

Before use, make sure that the sealing ring is securely fixed to the sealing ring rack and the anti-block shield is properly attached to the vapor discharge pipe.

A properly fitted sealing ring can be moved clockwise or counterclockwise in the sealing ring rack with little force.

With instant pots, the whole family can cook meals in less than 30 minutes. Cooked dishes such as rice, chicken, beef stew, sauce, yakitori can be cooked for 30-60 minutes from the beginning to the end. And yes, you can bake bread in an instant pot.

Old and ketogenic diet fans love instant pots for their ability to `` roast " meat in such a short time, but vegetarians and vegans that can quickly cook dishes such as pumpkin soup, baked potatoes and marinated potato chilis, also highly appreciated oatmeal cream and macaroni and cheese.

Even dried beans, which usually require overnight cooking, can be prepared in 30 minutes to make spicy hummus.

Broccoli Snackers

Preparation Time: 10 minutes

Cooking Time: 12 minutes

Servings: 4

Ingredients:

1 large head of broccoli, chopped into florets

1 tablespoon olive oil

1/2 teaspoon salt

Directions:

Preheat instant pot at 350°F for 3 minutes.

In a large bowl, toss broccoli florets with olive oil.

Place half of broccoli in fryer basket. Cook 3

minutes. Shake. Cook an additional 3 minutes.

Transfer to a serving bowl. Season with salt.

Repeat with remaining broccoli and serve warm.

Nutrition:

Calories: 81

Fat: 3.4 g

Protein: 4.3 g

Sodium: 340 mg

Fiber: 4.0 g

Carbohydrates: 10.1 g

Sugar: 2.6 g

Bite-Sized Pork Egg Rolls

Preparation Time: 30 minutes

Cooking Time: 24 minutes

Servings: 10

Ingredients:

1/2-pound lean ground pork

2 cups coleslaw mix (shredded cabbage and carrots)

3 scallions, trimmed and minced

1 tablespoon hoisin sauce

1 tablespoon soy sauce

1/4 teaspoon sriracha

1/2 teaspoon lime juice

30 wonton wrappers

2 teaspoons olive oil

Directions:

In a large skillet, heat ground pork over medium-high heat. Stir-fry 5–6 minutes until no longer pink. Add coleslaw mix and stir into pork. Add scallions, hoisin sauce, soy sauce, sriracha, and lime juice. Stir-fry an additional 2 minutes. Remove from heat and let rest 5 minutes off the burner.

Place a wonton wrapper on a cutting board. Place a small bowl of water near the board. Spoon approximately 2 teaspoons mixture in a line in the middle of the wrapper. Dip your finger into the water and lightly run it around the perimeter of the wonton wrapper. Fold 1/4" of the perimeter of wonton toward the middle. Roll up the length to form an egg roll. Repeat for each wonton wrapper. Preheat instant pot at 325°F for 3 minutes.

Place half of the egg rolls in the instant pot basket. Cook 3 minutes. Lightly brush the tops of egg rolls with olive oil. Cook an additional 5 minutes. Repeat with second batch.

Transfer to a plate. Serve warm.

Nutrition:

Calories: 106

Fat: 1.2 g

Protein: 7.5 g

Sodium: 268 mg

Fiber: 0.9 g

Carbohydrates: 15.7 g

Sugar: 1.0 g

Green Chili Crispy Wonton Squares

Preparation Time: 15 minutes

Cooking Time: 35 minutes

Servings: 6

Ingredients:

30 wonton wrappers

1 cup refried beans

2 (4-ounce) cans diced green chilies

1 cup grated queso fresco

Directions:

Place a wonton wrapper on a cutting board. Place approximately 11/2 teaspoons beans in the middle of wrapper. Add approximately 11/2 teaspoons green chilies and approximately 11/2 teaspoons queso fresco.

Place a small bowl of water near the working area. Dip your finger in the water bowl and run it around the perimeter of the wonton. Bring all corners to the center and press the straight edges together. Set aside. Repeat with remaining wontons.

Preheat instant pot at 325°F for 3 minutes.

Place six wontons in instant pot basket. Cook 7 minutes. Transfer to a plate and cook the remaining batches. Serve warm.

Nutrition:

Calories: 220

Fat: 4.8 g

Protein: 9.7 g

Sodium: 680 mg

Fiber: 3.9 g

Carbohydrates: 31.7 g

Sugar: 2.0 g

Brie And Red Pepper Jelly Triangles

Preparation Time: 10 minutes

Cooking Time: 16 minutes

Servings: 4

Ingredients:

20 wonton wrappers

10 teaspoons Brie cheese

10 teaspoons red pepper jelly

40 almond slivers

1 tablespoon olive oil

Directions:

Place a wonton wrapper on a cutting board. Place approximately 1/2 teaspoon Brie and then 1/2 teaspoon red pepper jelly in the middle of wrapper. Place 2 almond slivers on top.

Place a small bowl of water near the working area. Dip your finger in the water bowl and run it around the perimeter of the wonton. Fold one corner to the opposite corner, forming a triangle. Press down edges to seal. Set aside. Repeat with remaining wontons.

Preheat instant pot at 325°F for 3 minutes.

Place half of the triangles in the instant pot basket. Cook 3 minutes. Lightly brush the tops of triangles with olive oil. Cook an additional 5 minutes. Repeat with second batch.

Transfer to a plate. Serve warm.

Nutrition:

Calories: 239

Fat: 8.9 g

Protein: 6.9 g

Sodium: 292 mg

Fiber: 1.6 g

Carbohydrates: 32.2 g

Sugar: 7.8 g

Reuben Pizza For One

Preparation Time: 10 minutes

Cooking Time: 17 minutes

Servings: 1

Ingredients:

1/4-pound fresh pizza dough, about the size of a tennis ball

1/4 teaspoon caraway seeds

2 tablespoons Thousand Island dressing (or Russian dressing)

1/4 cup chopped corned beef

1/4 cup shredded Swiss cheese

1/4 cup sauerkraut, drained

Directions:

Preheat instant pot at 200°F for 6 minutes.

Press out dough to fit pizza pan (accessory).

Sprinkle caraway seeds evenly over dough. Cook 7 minutes.

Turn up the heat to 275°F.

Remove basket and spread dressing over dough, leaving 1/4" outer crust uncovered. Evenly add corned beef. Sprinkle cheese over meat. Cook an additional 10 minutes.

Gently transfer pizza to a cutting board. Evenly add sauerkraut. Cut into six slices and serve.

Nutrition:

Calories: 848

Fat: 42.5 g

Protein: 41.3 g

Sodium: 2,409 mg

Fiber: 3.1 g

Carbohydrates: 62.7 g

Sugar: 12.8 g

Parsnip Sticks

Preparation Time: 10 minutes

Cooking Time: 20 minutes

Servings: 4

Ingredients:

1 pound parsnips, peeled and cut into sticks

Salt and black pepper to the taste

2 tablespoons butter, melted

Juice of 1 lime

1 teaspoon mint, dried

1 teaspoon rosemary, dried

Directions:

In the instant pot's basket, mix the parsnip sticks with the melted butter and the other ingredients, toss, cook at 320 degrees F for 20 minutes and serve as a snack.

Nutrition:

Calories 40

Fat 3

Fiber 7

Carbs 3

Protein 7

Turmeric Sweet Potato Bites

Preparation Time: 10 minutes

Cooking Time: 25 minutes

Servings: 4

Ingredients:

2 sweet potatoes, peeled and roughly cubed

1 tablespoon olive oil

½ teaspoon sweet paprika

1 teaspoon turmeric powder

1 tablespoon chives, chopped

Salt and black pepper to the taste

Directions:

In the instant pot's basket, mix the potato bites with the oil, paprika and the other ingredients, toss and cook at 380 degrees F for 25 minutes, shaking the fryer from time to time.

Serve as a snack right away.

Nutrition:

Calories 161

Fat 1

Fiber 2

Carbs 5

Protein 3

Avocado Balls

Preparation Time: 10 minutes

Cooking Time: 16 minutes

Servings: 6

Ingredients:

10 oz. ground beef

1/3 teaspoon salt

1 onion, diced

1 avocado, pitted, peeled

½ teaspoon ground black pepper

1 tablespoon avocado oil

Directions:

Blend the avocado and put it in the bowl.

Add ground beef and salt.

After this, add the diced onion and ground black pepper.

Stir the ground beef mixture until homogenous.

Make the medium balls from the mixture and put them in the instant pot basket.

Sprinkle the avocado balls with the oil and cook them for 16 minutes at 365 F.

Stir the avocado balls time to time with the help of a spatula.

Serve it!

Nutrition:

Calories 164

Fat 9.5

Fiber 2.7

Carbs 4.7

Protein 15.2

Hard-Boiled Egg Halves with Bacon

Preparation Time: 10 minutes

Cooking Time: 15 minutes

Servings: 6

Ingredients:

3 eggs

6 oz. bacon, chopped, cooked

1 teaspoon fresh parsley, chopped

1 teaspoon fresh dill, chopped

1 teaspoon olive oil

1 cherry tomato

Directions:

Put the eggs in the instant pot basket.

Cook the eggs for 15 minutes at 250 F.

Meanwhile, mix together the parsley, dill, and olive oil.

Chop the cherry tomato and add the green mixture.

Stir the mixture.

When the eggs are cooked – chill them and peel.

Cut the eggs into the halves.

Then place the bacon over the egg halves and add the green mixture.

Serve the appetizer immediately!

Nutrition:

Calories 192

Fat 14.8

Fiber 0

Carbs 0.7

Protein 13.3

Stuffed Figs with Almonds

Preparation Time: 10 minutes

Cooking Time: 5 minutes

Servings: 2

Ingredients:

2 figs, dried

1 oz. almonds

¾ teaspoon ground cinnamon

1 teaspoon fresh lemon juice

Directions:

Mix up together the ground cinnamon and lemon juice. Stir the mixture.

Make the cuts in the figs and fill with the ground cinnamon.

Add almonds and place in the instant pot basket.

Cook the figs for 5 minutes at 360 F.

Then chill the figs and serve!

Nutrition:

Calories 132

Fat 7.3

Fiber 4.1

Carbs 15.9

Protein 3.7

Pear Chips

Preparation Time: 10 minutes

Cooking Time: 25 minutes

Servings: 6

Ingredients:

3 pears

¾ teaspoon nutmeg

Directions:

Wash the pears and cut into the halves.

Remove the seeds and slice.

Place the sliced pears on the instant pot rack and sprinkle with the nutmeg.

Cook the pears for 25 minutes at 350 F.

Flip the sliced pears during cooking if desired.

Serve the cooked pear chips and enjoy!

Nutrition:

Calories 62

Fat 0.3

Fiber 3.3

Carbs 16.1

Protein 0.4

Peach Chips

Preparation Time: 8 minutes

Cooking Time: 6 minutes

Servings: 6

Ingredients:

6 peaches

¼ teaspoon ground cinnamon

1 teaspoon water

Directions:

Remove the stones from the peaches.

Sprinkle peaches with the ground cinnamon and water.

Then place the peaches on the instant pot rack.

Cook the peaches for 15 minutes at 380 F.

When the time is over – remove the cooked chips from the instant pot and chill well.

Serve.

Nutrition:

Calories 59

Fat 0.4

Fiber 2.4

Carbs 14.1

Protein 1.4

Garlic Tomato Circles

Preparation Time: 10 minutes

Cooking Time: 20 minutes

Servings: 4

Ingredients:

2 tomatoes

¼ teaspoon salt

1 garlic clove, chopped

1 teaspoon olive oil

¾ teaspoon chili flakes

Directions:

Slice the tomatoes into the circles.

Then mix up together the chili flakes, olive oil,

salt, and chopped garlic.

Stir the mixture.

Rub the tomato circles with the oil mixture well.

Put the tomatoes on the instant pot rack and cook them for 20 minutes at 345 F.

Stir the tomatoes every 4 minutes.

When the time is over and the tomatoes are cooked – chill them well and serve!

Nutrition:

Calories 22

Fat 1.3

Fiber 0.8

Carbs 2.7

Protein 0.6

Beef Muffins

Preparation Time: 15 minutes

Cooking Time: 25 minutes

Servings: 6

Ingredients:

1 egg

10 oz. ground beef

1 tablespoon chives

1 teaspoon paprika

½ teaspoon chili flakes

1 tablespoon almond flour

¼ teaspoon salt

Directions:

Put the ground beef in the bowl and beat the egg in it.

Add paprika, chili flakes, and almond flour.

After this, add salt and stir it carefully.

Place the ground beef mixture in the muffin molds and put them in the instant pot.

Cook the beef muffins for 25 minutes at 360 F.

Then chill the beef muffins little and discard from the molds.

Serve!

Nutrition:

Calories 126

Fat 6.1

Fiber 0.6

Carbs 1.3

Protein 16.3

Trout Balls

Preparation Time: 10 minutes

Cooking Time: 8 minutes

Servings: 8

Ingredients:

10 oz. trout fillet

¼ teaspoon minced garlic

¼ teaspoon salt

1 teaspoon ground coriander

1 egg

2 tablespoons almond flour

1 teaspoon olive oil

1 teaspoon dried dill

Directions:

Chop the trout into the tiny pieces and combine it together with the minced garlic, salt, and ground coriander.

Beat the egg in the mixture and add almond flour and dried dill.

Stir it carefully until homogenous.

Make the small balls from the fish mixture with the help of 2 spoons.

Place the fish balls in the instant pot basket and sprinkle with the olive oil.

Cook the trout balls for 8 minutes at 380 F.

Chill the fish balls little and serve!

Nutrition:

Calories 121

Fat 7.7

Fiber 0.8

Carbs 1.6

Protein 11.7

Papaya Sticks

Preparation Time: 10 minutes

Cooking Time: 8 minutes

Servings: 2

Ingredients:

12 oz. papaya

1 tablespoon almond flour

1 teaspoon vanilla extract

Directions:

Peel the papaya and cut into the sticks.

Sprinkle the papaya sticks with the almond flour and vanilla extract.

Put the papaya sticks on the instant pot rack and cook them for 8 minutes at 380 F. Flip the papaya sticks on another side after 4 minutes of cooking.

Chill the cooked snack and serve!

Nutrition:

Calories 161

Fat 7.5

Fiber 4.5

Carbs 22.4

Protein 3.9

Broccoli Steaks

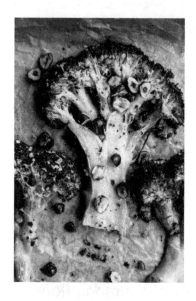

Preparation Time: 9 minutes

Cooking Time: 6 minutes

Servings: 4

Ingredients:

10 oz. broccoli head

1 tablespoon olive oil

¼ teaspoon turmeric

½ teaspoon salt

1 tablespoon almond flour

Directions:

Slice the broccoli into the steaks.

Sprinkle the broccoli steaks with the olive oil, turmeric, salt, and almond flour.

Stir them gently.

After this, put the broccoli in the instant pot basket and cook for 6 minutes at 400 F. Stir the broccoli steaks after 3 minutes.

Serve the cooked broccoli steak immediately!

Nutrition:
Calories 95

Fat 7.2

Fiber 2.6

Carbs 6.3

Protein 3.5

Devil Eggs with Pesto

Preparation Time: 10 minutes

Cooking Time: 15 minutes

Servings: 2

Ingredients:

2 eggs

1 cup fresh basil

¼ cup walnuts

2 tablespoons olive oil

¼ teaspoon salt

¼ teaspoon chili flakes

Directions:

Place the eggs on the instant pot rack and cook them at 250 F for 15 minutes.

Meanwhile, place the walnuts, olive oil, salt, and chili flakes in the blender.

Add the fresh basil and blend the mixture until smooth.

When the eggs are cooked – chill them and peel.

Cut the eggs into the halves and remove the egg whites.

Put the egg whites in the blender and blend the mixture for 30 seconds more.

Then fill the egg whites with the egg yolk pesto mixture.

Serve and enjoy!

Nutrition:

Calories 282

Fat 27.7

Fiber 1.3

Carbs 2.2

Protein 9.7

Crab Balls

Preparation Time: 5 minutes

Cooking Time: 20 minutes

Servings: 8

Ingredients:

½ cup coconut cream

2 tablespoons chives, mined

1 egg, whisked

1 teaspoon mustard

1 teaspoon lemon juice

16 ounces lump crabmeat, chopped

2/3 cup almond meal

A pinch of salt and black pepper

Cooking spray

Directions:

In a bowl, mix all the ingredients except the cooking spray and stir well.

Shape medium balls out of this mix, place them in the fryer and cook at 390 degrees F for 20 minutes.

Serve as an appetizer.

Nutrition:

Calories 141

Fat 7

Fiber 2

Carbs 4

Protein 9

365 Days Meal Plan

Days	Breakfast	Mains	Snacks
1	Acorn Squash	Pumpkin and Pork Escallops	Prosciutto-Wrapped Parmesan Asparagus
2	Instant Pot Air-Fried Avocado	Pork Curry with Cheese	Bacon-Wrapped Jalapeño Poppers
3	Mediterranea n Veggies In Instant Pot Air Fryer	Lemon and Pork Chops in Tomato Sauce	Garlic Parmesan Chicken Wings
4	Rosemary air-fried potatoes	Buckwheat with Pork Chunks	Spicy Buffalo Chicken Dip
5	Broccoli and Cauliflower Medley	Lime Pork with Pineapple and Peanuts	Bacon Jalapeño Cheese Bread

6	Roasted Squash Mix	Pork in Tomato Sauce with Pineapple	Pizza Rolls
7	Zucchini Satay	Pork in Tomato Sauce with Butter	Bacon Cheeseburger Dip
8	Cauliflower Cheese Pasta	Pork with Lemon	Pork Rind Tortillas
9	Pumpkin Baked Gnocchi	Spicy Pork Shoulder with Brown Rice	Mozzarella Sticks
10	Pumpkin Lasagna	Pork Ribs with Honey	Bacon-Wrapped Onion Rings
11	Haloumi Baked Rusti	Sausages Omelet with Bread and Peanuts	Mini Sweet Pepper Poppers
12	Celeriac Potato Gratin	Squash and Pork Chops	Spicy Spinach

			Artichoke Dip
13	Eggplant Pine Nut Roast	Pork Belly in Wine	Personal Mozzarella Pizza Crust
14	Roasted Veggie Casserole	Pork Meat and Pumpkin	Garlic Cheese Bread
15	Air Fryer Crispy Broccoli	Spicy Instant Pork with Peanuts	Crustless Three-Meat Pizza
16	Healthy Coconut Yogurt	Sunday Pot Roast	Bacon Snack
17	Oatmeal with Caramelized Bananas	One-Pot Pasta Bolognese	Shrimp Snack
18	Easy Homemade Oats	Five-Spice Boneless Beef Ribs	Avocado Wraps
19	Healthy Instant Oats with Fruit	Corned Beef	Cheesy Meatballs

20	Energetic Boiled Egg	Oxtail Ragu	Tuna Appetizer
21	Banana French Toast	Lamb Curry	Cheese And Leeks Dip
22	Delicious Scotch Eggs	Pulled Pork	Cucumber Salsa
23	Delicious Yogurt with Fruit	One-Pot Beans, Sausage, and Greens	Chicken Cubes
24	Breakfast Quinoa	Teriyaki Pork Loin	Salmon Spread
25	Easy Buckwheat Porridge	Easy Hawaiian-Style Pork	Crustless Pizza
26	Almond Steel-Cut Oatmeal	German Sausages with Peppers and Onions	Olives And Zucchini Cakes
27	Breakfast Mix	Beef Burgundy	Fluffy Strawberry Muffins

28	Maple Pumpkin Steel-Cut Oatmeal	Beef Stroganoff With Spring Green Peas	Paleo Blueberry Muffins
29	Coffee Steel-Cut Oatmeal	Barbacoa Beef	Orange Cardamom Muffins With Coconut Butter Glaze
30	Vanilla Carrot Cake Oatmeal	Pot Roast with Carrots and Potatoes	Bacon And Egg Cups
31	Coconut Porridge	Sloppy Joes	Breadsticks
32	Easy Beef Sandwiches	Broccoli Beef	Butter Crackers
33	Raspberry Yogurt	Korean Beef Bowl	Homemade Almond Crackers
34	Chickpea & Avocado Burritos	Mongolian Beef And Broccoli	Pepperoni Chips

35	Easy Oatmeal Bowls with Raspberries	All-In-One Meatloaf with Mashed Potatoes	3-Ingredient Flourless Cheesy Breadsticks
36	Super-Fast Pomegranate Porridge	Hawaiian Pineapple Pork	Cauliflower Breadsticks
37	Chicken Sandwiches with BBQ Sauce	Pork Carnitas	Breadsticks With Mozzarella Dough
38	Squash Tart Oatmeal	Sweet and Sour Pork	Bacon Onion Cookies
39	Cherry Oatmeal	Tangy Vinegar Pork with Potatoes	Cinnamon Swirl Cookies
40	Mushroom & Cheese Oatmeal	Polish Sausage with Sauerkraut	Peanut Butter Cookies

41	Egg Croissants	Spicy Lamb Shoulder with Bulgur	Cranberry Pistachio Vegan Shortbread Cookies
42	Broccoli Egg Morning	Beef Ribs with Lamb and Honey	Garlic Edamame
43	Broccoli Cheese Omelet	Lamb Sausages with Shrimps and Noodles	Spicy Chickpeas
44	Jar Breakfast	Spicy Lamb and Bean Rice	Black Bean Corn Dip
45	Vanilla Peach Oats	Spicy Lamb with Garlic and Mustard	Crunchy Tex-Mex Tortilla Chips
46	Pecan Pie Oatmeal	President Pork with Peanuts	Egg Roll Pizza Sticks

47	Berry Chia Oats	Pork with Apricots, Raisins and Pistachios	Cajun Zucchini Chips
48	Potato Ham Breakfast Casserole	Lamb and Zucchini	Mexican Potato Skins
49	Boiled Eggs	Spicy Rendang Lamb and Beef with Lemon	Crispy Old Bay Chicken Wings
50	Ham Sausage Quiche	Lamb and Beef with Limes	Cinnamon and Sugar Peaches
51	Millet Porridge	Lamb with Pineapple	Spicy Dill Pickle Fries
52	Chia Spiced Rice Pudding	Orange and Lamb Chops in Tomato Sauce with Red Carrots	Carrot Chips

53	Cheesy Bacon Oats	Lamb and Turkey	Spicy Corn On The Cob
54	Crunchy Cinnamon Toast Rice Pudding	Instant Lamb Steak with Apples and Pears	Pickle Chips
55	Bacon Egg Mystery Muffins	Adobo Chicken	Beet Chips
56	Morning Sweet Potato Breakfast Bowls	Tomato & Feta Shrimp	Potato Chips
57	Optimum Chicken and Apple Meatballs	Roasted Chicken	Dehydrated Coconut Wrap
58	Gratifying Kale Butternut Squash and Pancetta	Salsa Chicken	Dehydrated Banana Chips

	Breakfast Hash		
59	Palatable Maple Bacon Banana Breakfast Muffins	Citrus Herb Chicken	Dehydrated Banana Candy
60	Highly Regarded Cauliflower and Sweet Potato Breakfast Hash	Italian Shredded Chicken	Garlic Jerky
61	Instant Pot Asparagus and Goat Cheese Frittatas	Zoodle Soup	Sweet & Tangy Mango Slices
62	Instant Pot Black Rice Pudding	Mojo Chicken	Dehydrated Bananas

63	Broccoli Frittata with Ham and Peppers	Chinese BBQ Pork (Char Siu)	Canned Peaches
64	Instant Pot Chocolate Quinoa Breakfast Bowl	Korean Pork Ribs (Dwaeji Galbi Jjim)	Peach Wedges
65	Corn Meal Porridge in Instant Pot	Pork Ribs with Black Beans (Chinese)	Cinnamon Apple Chips
66	Eggs and Cocotte in the Instant Pot	Vietnamese Braised Pork Belly (Thit Kho tau)	Green Apple Chips
67	Instant Pot Ground Corn Breakfast Bowls	Malaysian Beef Rendang	Sliced Strawberries
68	Instant Pot Apple	Beef Caldereta	Dried Raspberries

	Cinnamon French Toast Casserole		
69	Instant Pot Banana Bread	Filipino BBQ Ribs	Bite-Sized Blooming Onions
70	Instant Pot Breakfast Burritos	Pilipino Kare Kare	Mini Scotch Eggs
71	Instant Pot Breakfast Potatoes	Filipino Beef Tapa	Pimiento Cheese-Stuffed Jalapeños
72	Instant Pot Chocolate Chip Banana Bread Bites	Korean Short Ribs	Jalapeño Popper Bombs
73	Instant Pot Congee	Lemon Grass Quinoa	Cheddar Biscuit-Breaded Green Olives

74	Instant Pot Easy Poached Egg	Pumpkin, Walnut Chili	Fried Feta-Dill-Breaded Kalamata Olives
75	Instant Pot Khaman Dhokla Recipe	Cauliflower Quiche with Goat's Cheese	Buffalo-Honey Chicken Wings
76	Sausage Egg Breakfast	Crustless Sweet Potato Quiche	Peanut Butter And Strawberry Jelly Wings
77	Stuffed Breakfast Peppers	Cauliflower Casserole	Thai Sweet Chili Wings
78	Healthy Ham Egg Omelet	Ratatouille	Salmon Croquettes
79	Mushroom Frittata	Mac and Cheese	Pepperoni Pizza Bites
80	Spinach Bacon Quiche	Cauliflower Chickpea Curry	Broccoli Snackers

81	Roasted Potato Cubes	Wild Rice and Basmati Pilaf	Bite-Sized Pork Egg Rolls
82	Cheese Eggs Breakfast	Feta Dill Sweet Potato Mash	Green Chili Crispy Wonton Squares
83	Breakfast Salmon Patties	Chili Garlic Noodles	Brie And Red Pepper Jelly Triangles
84	Zucchini Fries	Walnut Lentil Tacos	Reuben Pizza For One
85	Breakfast Stuffed Peppers	Penne Rigate	Parsnip Sticks
86	Crispy Breakfast Potatoes	Spinach Pasta	Turmeric Sweet Potato Bites
87	Quick Cheese Omelet	Pasta with Cranberry Beans	Avocado Balls

---

88	Tomato Spinach Frittata	Cheddar Haddock	Hard-Boiled Egg Halves with Bacon
89	Roasted Brussels Sprouts & Sweet Potatoes	Shrimp Curry	Stuffed Figs with Almonds
90	Roasted Potato wedges	Sweet & Sour Fish	Pear Chips
91	Breakfast Egg Bites	Lemon Dijon Tilapia	Peach Chips
92	Acorn Squash	Shrimp & Ricotta Recipe	Garlic Tomato Circles
93	Instant Pot Air-Fried Avocado	Scallop Coconut Curry	Beef Muffins
94	Mediterranea n Veggies In Instant Pot Air Fryer	Cheesy Pork Bites	Trout Balls

95	Rosemary air-fried potatoes	Spicy Honey Chicken	Papaya Sticks
96	Broccoli and Cauliflower Medley	Curry with Zucchini	Broccoli Steaks
97	Roasted Squash Mix	Beef Stew	Devil Eggs with Pesto
98	Zucchini Satay	Cheesy Beef Pie	Crab Balls
99	Cauliflower Cheese Pasta	Wine Chicken Pasta	Prosciutto-Wrapped Parmesan Asparagus
100	Pumpkin Baked Gnocchi	Beef Lasagna	Bacon-Wrapped Jalapeño Poppers
101	Pumpkin Lasagna	Garlic & Spinach Pasta	Garlic Parmesan Chicken Wings

102	Haloumi Baked Rusti	Noodle Cream Chicken	Spicy Buffalo Chicken Dip
103	Celeriac Potato Gratin	Sweet BBQ Chicken Wings	Bacon Jalapeño Cheese Bread
104	Eggplant Pine Nut Roast	Rosemary Wine Chicken	Pizza Rolls
105	Roasted Veggie Casserole	Spicy Beef with Garlic and Mayonnaise	Bacon Cheeseburger Dip
106	Air Fryer Crispy Broccoli	Beef Ragout	Pork Rind Tortillas
107	Healthy Coconut Yogurt	Spicy and Sour Pork Ribs	Mozzarella Sticks
108	Oatmeal with Caramelized Bananas	Spiced Pork Chops	Bacon-Wrapped Onion Rings

109	Easy Homemade Oats	Lamb Stew with Bacon	Mini Sweet Pepper Poppers
110	Healthy Instant Oats with Fruit	Beef with Pineapples, Raisins, and Pistachios	Spicy Spinach Artichoke Dip
111	Energetic Boiled Egg	Instant Goose with Herbs and Madeira	Personal Mozzarella Pizza Crust
112	Banana French Toast	Flavorful Spaghetti	Garlic Cheese Bread
113	Delicious Scotch Eggs	Jerk Chicken & Rice	Crustless Three-Meat Pizza
114	Delicious Yogurt with Fruit	Tasty Cream Cheese Risotto	Bacon Snack
115	Breakfast Quinoa	Easy Coconut Rice	Shrimp Snack

116	Easy Buckwheat Porridge	Chicken Cheese Pasta	Avocado Wraps
117	Almond Steel-Cut Oatmeal	Tasty Cheeseburger Macaroni	Cheesy Meatballs
118	Breakfast Mix	Quick Cheese Macaroni	Tuna Appetizer
119	Maple Pumpkin Steel-Cut Oatmeal	Delicious Creamy Ziti	Cheese And Leeks Dip
120	Coffee Steel-Cut Oatmeal	Perfect Alfredo	Cucumber Salsa
121	Vanilla Carrot Cake Oatmeal	Simple Tomato Rice	Chicken Cubes
122	Coconut Porridge	Mushroom Pea Risotto	Salmon Spread
123	Easy Beef Sandwiches	Vegetable Parmesan Risotto	Crustless Pizza

124	Raspberry Yogurt	Parmesan Shrimp Risotto	Olives And Zucchini Cakes
125	Chickpea & Avocado Burritos	Basil Tomato Risotto	Fluffy Strawberry Muffins
126	Easy Oatmeal Bowls with Raspberries	Healthy Veggie Pasta	Paleo Blueberry Muffins
127	Super-Fast Pomegranate Porridge	Pumpkin and Pork Escallops	Orange Cardamom Muffins With Coconut Butter Glaze
128	Chicken Sandwiches with BBQ Sauce	Pork Curry with Cheese	Bacon And Egg Cups
129	Squash Tart Oatmeal	Lemon and Pork Chops in Tomato Sauce	Breadsticks

130	Cherry Oatmeal	Buckwheat with Pork Chunks	Butter Crackers
131	Mushroom & Cheese Oatmeal	Lime Pork with Pineapple and Peanuts	Homemade Almond Crackers
132	Egg Croissants	Pork in Tomato Sauce with Pineapple	Pepperoni Chips
133	Broccoli Egg Morning	Pork in Tomato Sauce with Butter	3-Ingredient Flourless Cheesy Breadsticks
134	Broccoli Cheese Omelet	Pork with Lemon	Cauliflower Breadsticks
135	Jar Breakfast	Spicy Pork Shoulder with Brown Rice	Breadsticks With Mozzarella Dough

136	Vanilla Peach Oats	Pork Ribs with Honey	Bacon Onion Cookies
137	Pecan Pie Oatmeal	Sausages Omelet with Bread and Peanuts	Cinnamon Swirl Cookies
138	Berry Chia Oats	Squash and Pork Chops	Peanut Butter Cookies
139	Potato Ham Breakfast Casserole	Pork Belly in Wine	Cranberry Pistachio Vegan Shortbread Cookies
140	Boiled Eggs	Pork Meat and Pumpkin	Garlic Edamame
141	Ham Sausage Quiche	Spicy Instant Pork with Peanuts	Spicy Chickpeas
142	Millet Porridge	Sunday Pot Roast	Black Bean Corn Dip

143	Chia Spiced Rice Pudding	One-Pot Pasta Bolognese	Crunchy Tex-Mex Tortilla Chips
144	Cheesy Bacon Oats	Five-Spice Boneless Beef Ribs	Egg Roll Pizza Sticks
145	Crunchy Cinnamon Toast Rice Pudding	Corned Beef	Cajun Zucchini Chips
146	Bacon Egg Mystery Muffins	Oxtail Ragu	Mexican Potato Skins
147	Morning Sweet Potato Breakfast Bowls	Lamb Curry	Crispy Old Bay Chicken Wings
148	Optimum Chicken and Apple Meatballs	Pulled Pork	Cinnamon and Sugar Peaches

149	Gratifying Kale Butternut Squash and Pancetta Breakfast Hash	One-Pot Beans, Sausage, and Greens	Spicy Dill Pickle Fries
150	Palatable Maple Bacon Banana Breakfast Muffins	Teriyaki Pork Loin	Carrot Chips
151	Highly Regarded Cauliflower and Sweet Potato Breakfast Hash	Easy Hawaiian-Style Pork	Spicy Corn On The Cob
152	Instant Pot Asparagus and Goat	German Sausages with Peppers and Onions	Pickle Chips

	Cheese Frittatas		
153	Instant Pot Black Rice Pudding	Beef Burgundy	Beet Chips
154	Broccoli Frittata with Ham and Peppers	Beef Stroganoff With Spring Green Peas	Potato Chips
155	Instant Pot Chocolate Quinoa Breakfast Bowl	Barbacoa Beef	Dehydrated Coconut Wrap
156	Corn Meal Porridge in Instant Pot	Pot Roast with Carrots and Potatoes	Dehydrated Banana Chips
157	Eggs and Cocotte in the Instant Pot	Sloppy Joes	Dehydrated Banana Candy

158	Instant Pot Ground Corn Breakfast Bowls	Broccoli Beef	Garlic Jerky
159	Instant Pot Apple Cinnamon French Toast Casserole	Korean Beef Bowl	Sweet & Tangy Mango Slices
160	Instant Pot Banana Bread	Mongolian Beef And Broccoli	Dehydrated Bananas
161	Instant Pot Breakfast Burritos	All-In-One Meatloaf with Mashed Potatoes	Canned Peaches
162	Instant Pot Breakfast Potatoes	Hawaiian Pineapple Pork	Peach Wedges
163	Instant Pot Chocolate Chip Banana Bread Bites	Pork Carnitas	Cinnamon Apple Chips

164	Instant Pot Congee	Sweet and Sour Pork	Green Apple Chips
165	Instant Pot Easy Poached Egg	Tangy Vinegar Pork with Potatoes	Sliced Strawberries
166	Instant Pot Khaman Dhokla Recipe	Polish Sausage with Sauerkraut	Dried Raspberries
167	Sausage Egg Breakfast	Spicy Lamb Shoulder with Bulgur	Bite-Sized Blooming Onions
168	Stuffed Breakfast Peppers	Beef Ribs with Lamb and Honey	Mini Scotch Eggs
169	Healthy Ham Egg Omelet	Lamb Sausages with Shrimps and Noodles	Pimiento Cheese-Stuffed Jalapeños

170	Mushroom Frittata	Spicy Lamb and Bean Rice	Jalapeño Popper Bombs
171	Spinach Bacon Quiche	Spicy Lamb with Garlic and Mustard	Cheddar Biscuit-Breaded Green Olives
172	Roasted Potato Cubes	President Pork with Peanuts	Fried Feta-Dill-Breaded Kalamata Olives
173	Cheese Eggs Breakfast	Pork with Apricots, Raisins and Pistachios	Buffalo-Honey Chicken Wings
174	Breakfast Salmon Patties	Lamb and Zucchini	Peanut Butter And Strawberry Jelly Wings
175	Zucchini Fries	Spicy Rendang Lamb and	Thai Sweet Chili Wings

		Beef with Lemon	
176	Breakfast Stuffed Peppers	Lamb and Beef with Limes	Salmon Croquettes
177	Crispy Breakfast Potatoes	Lamb with Pineapple	Pepperoni Pizza Bites
178	Quick Cheese Omelet	Orange and Lamb Chops in Tomato Sauce with Red Carrots	Broccoli Snackers
179	Tomato Spinach Frittata	Lamb and Turkey	Bite-Sized Pork Egg Rolls
180	Roasted Brussels Sprouts & Sweet Potatoes	Instant Lamb Steak with Apples and Pears	Green Chili Crispy Wonton Squares

181	Roasted Potato wedges	Adobo Chicken	Brie And Red Pepper Jelly Triangles
182	Breakfast Egg Bites	Tomato & Feta Shrimp	Reuben Pizza For One
183	Acorn Squash	Roasted Chicken	Parsnip Sticks
184	Instant Pot Air-Fried Avocado	Salsa Chicken	Turmeric Sweet Potato Bites
185	Mediterranea n Veggies In Instant Pot Air Fryer	Citrus Herb Chicken	Avocado Balls
186	Rosemary air-fried potatoes	Italian Shredded Chicken	Hard-Boiled Egg Halves with Bacon
187	Broccoli and Cauliflower Medley	Zoodle Soup	Stuffed Figs with Almonds

188	Roasted Squash Mix	Mojo Chicken	Pear Chips
189	Zucchini Satay	Chinese BBQ Pork (Char Siu)	Peach Chips
190	Cauliflower Cheese Pasta	Korean Pork Ribs (Dwaeji Galbi Jjim)	Garlic Tomato Circles
191	Pumpkin Baked Gnocchi	Pork Ribs with Black Beans (Chinese)	Beef Muffins
192	Pumpkin Lasagna	Vietnamese Braised Pork Belly (Thit Kho tau)	Trout Balls
193	Haloumi Baked Rusti	Malaysian Beef Rendang	Papaya Sticks
194	Celeriac Potato Gratin	Beef Caldereta	Broccoli Steaks

195	Eggplant Pine Nut Roast	Filipino BBQ Ribs	Devil Eggs with Pesto
196	Roasted Veggie Casserole	Pilipino Kare Kare	Crab Balls
197	Air Fryer Crispy Broccoli	Filipino Beef Tapa	Prosciutto-Wrapped Parmesan Asparagus
198	Healthy Coconut Yogurt	Korean Short Ribs	Bacon-Wrapped Jalapeño Poppers
199	Oatmeal with Caramelized Bananas	Lemon Grass Quinoa	Garlic Parmesan Chicken Wings
200	Easy Homemade Oats	Pumpkin, Walnut Chili	Spicy Buffalo Chicken Dip

201	Healthy Instant Oats with Fruit	Cauliflower Quiche with Goat's Cheese	Bacon Jalapeño Cheese Bread
202	Energetic Boiled Egg	Crustless Sweet Potato Quiche	Pizza Rolls
203	Banana French Toast	Cauliflower Casserole	Bacon Cheeseburg er Dip
204	Delicious Scotch Eggs	Ratatouille	Pork Rind Tortillas
205	Delicious Yogurt with Fruit	Mac and Cheese	Mozzarella Sticks
206	Breakfast Quinoa	Cauliflower Chickpea Curry	Bacon-Wrapped Onion Rings
207	Easy Buckwheat Porridge	Wild Rice and Basmati Pilaf	Mini Sweet Pepper Poppers

208	Almond Steel-Cut Oatmeal	Feta Dill Sweet Potato Mash	Spicy Spinach Artichoke Dip
209	Breakfast Mix	Chili Garlic Noodles	Personal Mozzarella Pizza Crust
210	Maple Pumpkin Steel-Cut Oatmeal	Walnut Lentil Tacos	Garlic Cheese Bread
211	Coffee Steel-Cut Oatmeal	Penne Rigate	Crustless Three-Meat Pizza
212	Vanilla Carrot Cake Oatmeal	Spinach Pasta	Bacon Snack
213	Coconut Porridge	Pasta with Cranberry Beans	Shrimp Snack
214	Easy Beef Sandwiches	Cheddar Haddock	Avocado Wraps

215	Raspberry Yogurt	Shrimp Curry	Cheesy Meatballs
216	Chickpea & Avocado Burritos	Sweet & Sour Fish	Tuna Appetizer
217	Easy Oatmeal Bowls with Raspberries	Lemon Dijon Tilapia	Cheese And Leeks Dip
218	Super-Fast Pomegranate Porridge	Shrimp & Ricotta Recipe	Cucumber Salsa
219	Chicken Sandwiches with BBQ Sauce	Scallop Coconut Curry	Chicken Cubes
220	Squash Tart Oatmeal	Cheesy Pork Bites	Salmon Spread
221	Cherry Oatmeal	Spicy Honey Chicken	Crustless Pizza
222	Mushroom & Cheese Oatmeal	Curry with Zucchini	Olives And Zucchini Cakes

223	Egg Croissants	Beef Stew	Fluffy Strawberry Muffins
224	Broccoli Egg Morning	Cheesy Beef Pie	Paleo Blueberry Muffins
225	Broccoli Cheese Omelet	Wine Chicken Pasta	Orange Cardamom Muffins With Coconut Butter Glaze
226	Jar Breakfast	Beef Lasagna	Bacon And Egg Cups
227	Vanilla Peach Oats	Garlic & Spinach Pasta	Breadsticks
228	Pecan Pie Oatmeal	Noodle Cream Chicken	Butter Crackers
229	Berry Chia Oats	Sweet BBQ Chicken Wings	Homemade Almond Crackers

230	Potato Ham Breakfast Casserole	Rosemary Wine Chicken	Pepperoni Chips
231	Boiled Eggs	Spicy Beef with Garlic and Mayonnaise	3-Ingredient Flourless Cheesy Breadsticks
232	Ham Sausage Quiche	Beef Ragout	Cauliflower Breadsticks
223	Millet Porridge	Spicy and Sour Pork Ribs	Breadsticks With Mozzarella Dough
234	Chia Spiced Rice Pudding	Spiced Pork Chops	Bacon Onion Cookies
235	Cheesy Bacon Oats	Lamb Stew with Bacon	Cinnamon Swirl Cookies
236	Crunchy Cinnamon Toast Rice Pudding	Beef with Pineapples, Raisins, and Pistachios	Peanut Butter Cookies

237	Bacon Egg Mystery Muffins	Instant Goose with Herbs and Madeira	Cranberry Pistachio Vegan Shortbread Cookies
238	Morning Sweet Potato Breakfast Bowls	Flavorful Spaghetti	Garlic Edamame
239	Optimum Chicken and Apple Meatballs	Jerk Chicken & Rice	Spicy Chickpeas
240	Gratifying Kale Butternut Squash and Pancetta Breakfast Hash	Tasty Cream Cheese Risotto	Black Bean Corn Dip
241	Palatable Maple Bacon Banana	Easy Coconut Rice	Crunchy Tex-Mex

	Breakfast Muffins		Tortilla Chips
242	Highly Regarded Cauliflower and Sweet Potato Breakfast Hash	Chicken Cheese Pasta	Egg Roll Pizza Sticks
243	Instant Pot Asparagus and Goat Cheese Frittatas	Tasty Cheeseburger Macaroni	Cajun Zucchini Chips
244	Instant Pot Black Rice Pudding	Quick Cheese Macaroni	Mexican Potato Skins
245	Broccoli Frittata with Ham and Peppers	Delicious Creamy Ziti	Crispy Old Bay Chicken Wings

246	Instant Pot Chocolate Quinoa Breakfast Bowl	Perfect Alfredo	Cinnamon and Sugar Peaches
247	Corn Meal Porridge in Instant Pot	Simple Tomato Rice	Spicy Dill Pickle Fries
248	Eggs and Cocotte in the Instant Pot	Mushroom Pea Risotto	Carrot Chips
249	Instant Pot Ground Corn Breakfast Bowls	Vegetable Parmesan Risotto	Spicy Corn On The Cob
250	Instant Pot Apple Cinnamon French Toast Casserole	Parmesan Shrimp Risotto	Pickle Chips

251	Instant Pot Banana Bread	Basil Tomato Risotto	Beet Chips
252	Instant Pot Breakfast Burritos	Healthy Veggie Pasta	Potato Chips
253	Instant Pot Breakfast Potatoes	Pumpkin and Pork Escallops	Dehydrated Coconut Wrap
254	Instant Pot Chocolate Chip Banana Bread Bites	Pork Curry with Cheese	Dehydrated Banana Chips
255	Instant Pot Congee	Lemon and Pork Chops in Tomato Sauce	Dehydrated Banana Candy
256	Instant Pot Easy Poached Egg	Buckwheat with Pork Chunks	Garlic Jerky
257	Instant Pot Khaman	Lime Pork with	Sweet & Tangy

	Dhokla Recipe	Pineapple and Peanuts	Mango Slices
258	Sausage Egg Breakfast	Pork in Tomato Sauce with Pineapple	Dehydrated Bananas
259	Stuffed Breakfast Peppers	Pork in Tomato Sauce with Butter	Canned Peaches
260	Healthy Ham Egg Omelet	Pork with Lemon	Peach Wedges
261	Mushroom Frittata	Spicy Pork Shoulder with Brown Rice	Cinnamon Apple Chips
262	Spinach Bacon Quiche	Pork Ribs with Honey	Green Apple Chips
263	Roasted Potato Cubes	Sausages Omelet with Bread and Peanuts	Sliced Strawberries

264	Cheese Eggs Breakfast	Squash and Pork Chops	Dried Raspberries
265	Breakfast Salmon Patties	Pork Belly in Wine	Bite-Sized Blooming Onions
266	Zucchini Fries	Pork Meat and Pumpkin	Mini Scotch Eggs
267	Breakfast Stuffed Peppers	Spicy Instant Pork with Peanuts	Pimiento Cheese- Stuffed Jalapeños
268	Crispy Breakfast Potatoes	Sunday Pot Roast	Jalapeño Popper Bombs
269	Quick Cheese Omelet	One-Pot Pasta Bolognese	Cheddar Biscuit- Breaded Green Olives
270	Tomato Spinach Frittata	Five-Spice Boneless Beef Ribs	Fried Feta- Dill-Breaded Kalamata Olives

271	Roasted Brussels Sprouts & Sweet Potatoes	Corned Beef	Buffalo-Honey Chicken Wings
272	Roasted Potato wedges	Oxtail Ragu	Peanut Butter And Strawberry Jelly Wings
273	Breakfast Egg Bites	Lamb Curry	Thai Sweet Chili Wings
274	Acorn Squash	Pulled Pork	Salmon Croquettes
275	Instant Pot Air-Fried Avocado	One-Pot Beans, Sausage, and Greens	Pepperoni Pizza Bites
276	Mediterranean Veggies In Instant Pot Air Fryer	Teriyaki Pork Loin	Broccoli Snackers

277	Rosemary air-fried potatoes	Easy Hawaiian-Style Pork	Bite-Sized Pork Egg Rolls
278	Broccoli and Cauliflower Medley	German Sausages with Peppers and Onions	Green Chili Crispy Wonton Squares
279	Roasted Squash Mix	Beef Burgundy	Brie And Red Pepper Jelly Triangles
280	Zucchini Satay	Beef Stroganoff With Spring Green Peas	Reuben Pizza For One
281	Cauliflower Cheese Pasta	Barbacoa Beef	Parsnip Sticks
282	Pumpkin Baked Gnocchi	Pot Roast with Carrots and Potatoes	Turmeric Sweet Potato Bites
283	Pumpkin Lasagna	Sloppy Joes	Avocado Balls

284	Haloumi Baked Rusti	Broccoli Beef	Hard-Boiled Egg Halves with Bacon
285	Celeriac Potato Gratin	Korean Beef Bowl	Stuffed Figs with Almonds
286	Eggplant Pine Nut Roast	Mongolian Beef And Broccoli	Pear Chips
287	Roasted Veggie Casserole	All-In-One Meatloaf with Mashed Potatoes	Peach Chips
288	Air Fryer Crispy Broccoli	Hawaiian Pineapple Pork	Garlic Tomato Circles
289	Healthy Coconut Yogurt	Pork Carnitas	Beef Muffins
290	Oatmeal with Caramelized Bananas	Sweet and Sour Pork	Trout Balls

291	Easy Homemade Oats	Tangy Vinegar Pork with Potatoes	Papaya Sticks
292	Healthy Instant Oats with Fruit	Polish Sausage with Sauerkraut	Broccoli Steaks
293	Energetic Boiled Egg	Spicy Lamb Shoulder with Bulgur	Devil Eggs with Pesto
294	Banana French Toast	Beef Ribs with Lamb and Honey	Crab Balls
295	Delicious Scotch Eggs	Lamb Sausages with Shrimps and Noodles	Prosciutto-Wrapped Parmesan Asparagus
296	Delicious Yogurt with Fruit	Spicy Lamb and Bean Rice	Bacon-Wrapped Jalapeño Poppers

297	Breakfast Quinoa	Spicy Lamb with Garlic and Mustard	Garlic Parmesan Chicken Wings
298	Easy Buckwheat Porridge	President Pork with Peanuts	Spicy Buffalo Chicken Dip
299	Almond Steel-Cut Oatmeal	Pork with Apricots, Raisins and Pistachios	Bacon Jalapeño Cheese Bread
300	Breakfast Mix	Lamb and Zucchini	Pizza Rolls
301	Maple Pumpkin Steel-Cut Oatmeal	Spicy Rendang Lamb and Beef with Lemon	Bacon Cheeseburger Dip
302	Coffee Steel-Cut Oatmeal	Lamb and Beef with Limes	Pork Rind Tortillas

303	Vanilla Carrot Cake Oatmeal	Lamb with Pineapple	Mozzarella Sticks
304	Coconut Porridge	Orange and Lamb Chops in Tomato Sauce with Red Carrots	Bacon-Wrapped Onion Rings
305	Easy Beef Sandwiches	Lamb and Turkey	Mini Sweet Pepper Poppers
306	Raspberry Yogurt	Instant Lamb Steak with Apples and Pears	Spicy Spinach Artichoke Dip
307	Chickpea & Avocado Burritos	Adobo Chicken	Personal Mozzarella Pizza Crust
308	Easy Oatmeal Bowls with Raspberries	Tomato & Feta Shrimp	Garlic Cheese Bread

309	Super-Fast Pomegranate Porridge	Roasted Chicken	Crustless Three-Meat Pizza
310	Chicken Sandwiches with BBQ Sauce	Salsa Chicken	Bacon Snack
311	Squash Tart Oatmeal	Citrus Herb Chicken	Shrimp Snack
312	Cherry Oatmeal	Italian Shredded Chicken	Avocado Wraps
313	Mushroom & Cheese Oatmeal	Zoodle Soup	Cheesy Meatballs
314	Egg Croissants	Mojo Chicken	Tuna Appetizer
315	Broccoli Egg Morning	Chinese BBQ Pork (Char Siu)	Cheese And Leeks Dip
316	Broccoli Cheese Omelet	Korean Pork Ribs (Dwaeji Galbi Jjim)	Cucumber Salsa

317	Jar Breakfast	Pork Ribs with Black Beans (Chinese)	Chicken Cubes
318	Vanilla Peach Oats	Vietnamese Braised Pork Belly (Thit Kho tau)	Salmon Spread
319	Pecan Pie Oatmeal	Malaysian Beef Rendang	Crustless Pizza
320	Berry Chia Oats	Beef Caldereta	Olives And Zucchini Cakes
321	Potato Ham Breakfast Casserole	Filipino BBQ Ribs	Fluffy Strawberry Muffins
322	Boiled Eggs	Pilipino Kare Kare	Paleo Blueberry Muffins
323	Ham Sausage Quiche	Filipino Beef Tapa	Orange Cardamom Muffins With

			Coconut Butter Glaze
324	Millet Porridge	Korean Short Ribs	Bacon And Egg Cups
325	Chia Spiced Rice Pudding	Lemon Grass Quinoa	Breadsticks
326	Cheesy Bacon Oats	Pumpkin, Walnut Chili	Butter Crackers
327	Crunchy Cinnamon Toast Rice Pudding	Cauliflower Quiche with Goat's Cheese	Homemade Almond Crackers
328	Bacon Egg Mystery Muffins	Crustless Sweet Potato Quiche	Pepperoni Chips
329	Morning Sweet Potato Breakfast Bowls	Cauliflower Casserole	3-Ingredient Flourless Cheesy Breadsticks
330	Optimum Chicken and	Ratatouille	Cauliflower Breadsticks

	Apple Meatballs		
331	Gratifying Kale Butternut Squash and Pancetta Breakfast Hash	Mac and Cheese	Breadsticks With Mozzarella Dough
332	Palatable Maple Bacon Banana Breakfast Muffins	Cauliflower Chickpea Curry	Bacon Onion Cookies
333	Highly Regarded Cauliflower and Sweet Potato Breakfast Hash	Wild Rice and Basmati Pilaf	Cinnamon Swirl Cookies

334	Instant Pot Asparagus and Goat Cheese Frittatas	Feta Dill Sweet Potato Mash	Peanut Butter Cookies
335	Instant Pot Black Rice Pudding	Chili Garlic Noodles	Cranberry Pistachio Vegan Shortbread Cookies
336	Broccoli Frittata with Ham and Peppers	Walnut Lentil Tacos	Garlic Edamame
337	Instant Pot Chocolate Quinoa Breakfast Bowl	Penne Rigate	Spicy Chickpeas
338	Corn Meal Porridge in Instant Pot	Spinach Pasta	Black Bean Corn Dip

339	Eggs and Cocotte in the Instant Pot	Pasta with Cranberry Beans	Crunchy Tex-Mex Tortilla Chips
340	Instant Pot Ground Corn Breakfast Bowls	Cheddar Haddock	Egg Roll Pizza Sticks
341	Instant Pot Apple Cinnamon French Toast Casserole	Shrimp Curry	Cajun Zucchini Chips
342	Instant Pot Banana Bread	Sweet & Sour Fish	Mexican Potato Skins
343	Instant Pot Breakfast Burritos	Lemon Dijon Tilapia	Crispy Old Bay Chicken Wings
344	Instant Pot Breakfast Potatoes	Shrimp & Ricotta Recipe	Cinnamon and Sugar Peaches

345	Instant Pot Chocolate Chip Banana Bread Bites	Scallop Coconut Curry	Spicy Dill Pickle Fries
346	Instant Pot Congee	Cheesy Pork Bites	Carrot Chips
347	Instant Pot Easy Poached Egg	Spicy Honey Chicken	Spicy Corn On The Cob
348	Instant Pot Khaman Dhokla Recipe	Curry with Zucchini	Pickle Chips
349	Sausage Egg Breakfast	Beef Stew	Beet Chips
350	Stuffed Breakfast Peppers	Cheesy Beef Pie	Potato Chips
351	Healthy Ham Egg Omelet	Wine Chicken Pasta	Dehydrated Coconut Wrap

352	Mushroom Frittata	Beef Lasagna	Dehydrated Banana Chips
353	Spinach Bacon Quiche	Garlic & Spinach Pasta	Dehydrated Banana Candy
354	Roasted Potato Cubes	Noodle Cream Chicken	Garlic Jerky
355	Cheese Eggs Breakfast	Sweet BBQ Chicken Wings	Sweet & Tangy Mango Slices
356	Breakfast Salmon Patties	Rosemary Wine Chicken	Dehydrated Bananas
357	Zucchini Fries	Spicy Beef with Garlic and Mayonnaise	Canned Peaches
358	Breakfast Stuffed Peppers	Beef Ragout	Peach Wedges

359	Crispy Breakfast Potatoes	Spicy and Sour Pork Ribs	Cinnamon Apple Chips
360	Quick Cheese Omelet	Spiced Pork Chops	Green Apple Chips
361	Tomato Spinach Frittata	Lamb Stew with Bacon	Sliced Strawberries
362	Roasted Brussels Sprouts & Sweet Potatoes	Beef with Pineapples, Raisins, and Pistachios	Dried Raspberries
363	Roasted Potato wedges	Instant Goose with Herbs and Madeira	Bite-Sized Blooming Onions
364	Breakfast Egg Bites	Flavorful Spaghetti	Mini Scotch Eggs
365	Acorn Squash	Jerk Chicken & Rice	Pimiento Cheese-

			Stuffed Jalapeños

Conclusion

When you are on a diet trying to lose weight or manage a condition, you will be strictly confined to follow an eating plan. Such plans often place numerous demands on individuals: food may need to be boiled, other foods are forbidden, permitting you only to eat small portions and so on.

On the other hand, a lifestyle such as the Mediterranean diet is entirely stress-free. It is easy to follow because there are almost no restrictions. There is no time limit on the Mediterranean diet because it is more of a lifestyle than a diet. You do not need to stop at some point but carry on for the rest of your life. The foods that you eat under the Mediterranean model include unrefined cereals, white meats, and the occasional dairy products.

The Mediterranean lifestyle, unlike other diets, also requires you to engage with family and friends and share meals together. It has been noted that communities around the Mediterranean spend between one and two hours enjoying their meals. This kind of bonding between family members or friends helps bring people closer together, which helps foster closer bonds hence fewer cases of depression, loneliness, or stress, all of which are precursors to chronic diseases.

You will achieve many benefits using the Instant Pot Pressure Cooker. These are just a few instances you will discover in your Mediterranean-style recipes:

Pressure cooking means that you can (on average) cook meals 75% faster than boiling/braising on the stovetop or baking and roasting in a conventional oven.

This is especially helpful for vegan meals that entail the use of dried beans, legumes, and pulses. Instead of pre-soaking these ingredients for hours before use, you can pour them directly into the Instant Pot, add water, and pressure cook these for several minutes. However, always follow your recipe carefully since they have been tested for accuracy.

Nutrients are preserved. You can use your pressure-cooking techniques using the Instant Pot to ensure the heat is evenly and quickly distributed.

It is not essential to immerse the food into the water. You will provide plenty of water in the cooker for efficient steaming. You will also be saving the essential vitamins and minerals. The food won't become oxidized by the exposure of air or heat. Enjoy those fresh green veggies with their natural and vibrant colors.

The cooking elements help keep the foods fully sealed, so the steam and aromas don't linger throughout your entire home. That is a plus, especially for items such as cabbage, which throws out a distinctive smell.

You will find that beans and whole grains will have a softer texture and will have an improved taste. The meal will be cooked consistently since the Instant Pot provides even heat distribution.

You'll also save tons of time and money. You will be using much less water, and the pot is fully insulated, making it more energy-efficient when compared to boiling or steaming your foods on the stovetop. It is also less expensive than using a microwave, not to mention how much more flavorful the food will be when prepared in the Instant Pot cooker.

You can delay the cooking of your food items so you can plan ahead of time. You won't need to stand around as you await your meal. You can reduce the cooking time by reducing the 'hands-on' time. Just leave for work or a day of activities, and you will come home to a special treat.

In a nutshell, the Instant Pot is:

Easy To Use Healthy recipes for the entire family are provided.

You can make authentic one-pot recipes in your Instant Pot.

If you forget to switch on your slow cooker, you can make any meal done in a few minutes in your Instant Pot.

You can securely and smoothly cook meat from frozen.

It's a laid-back way to cook. You don't have to watch a pan on the stove or a pot in the oven.

The pressure cooking procedure develops delicious flavors swiftly.